## Learning to Read, Step by Step!

**Ready to Read**   **Preschool–Kindergarten**
• big type and easy words • rhyme and rhythm • picture clues
For children who know the alphabet and are eager to
begin reading.

**Reading with Help**   **Preschool–Grade 1**
• basic vocabulary • short sentences • simple stories
For children who recognize familiar words and sound out
new words with help.

**Reading on Your Own**   **Grades 1–3**
• engaging characters • easy-to-follow plots • popular topics
For children who are ready to read on their own.

**Reading Paragraphs**   **Grades 2–3**
• challenging vocabulary • short paragraphs • exciting stories
For newly independent readers who read simple sentences
with confidence.

**Ready for Chapters**   **Grades 2–4**
• chapters • longer paragraphs • full-color art
For children who want to take the plunge into chapter books
but still like colorful pictures.

**STEP INTO READING®** is designed to give every child a successful
reading experience. The grade levels are only guides; children will progress
through the steps at their own speed, developing confidence in their reading.
Remember, a lifetime love of reading starts with a single step!

*To all the kids reading
(including Jack, Nate, Adelaide, Matt,
Gerard, Azzaria, and Amara)—
exactly as you are
—S.C.*

*To Marian Shields Robinson, Fraser C.
Robinson III, and all parents who inspire
their children to go high
—J.B.*

The editor would like to thank Michelle Gullion, Archives Director and Curator at the National First Ladies' Library, for her assistance in reviewing this text.

Text copyright © 2018 by Shana Corey
Illustrations copyright © 2018 by James Bernardin

Photograph credits: Cover: Getty Images/Paul Morigi for Fortune/Time Inc.; pp. 3 and 30: some rights reserved by Craig ONeal, found on Wikimedia Commons; pp. 32–33: some rights reserved by Tech. Sgt. Suzanne Day, USAF, found on Wikimedia Commons; pp. 38–39: USDA photo by Bob Nichols, found on Flickr Creative Commons; p. 40: Official White House Photo by Chuck Kennedy, found on Flickr Creative Commons; p. 41: photo by The White House, found on Wikimedia Commons; p. 43: some rights reserved by Steve Bott, found on Flickr Creative Commons; p. 45: photo by Simon Davis/DFID, found on Flickr Creative Commons; p. 46: USDA photo by Bob Nichols, found on Flickr Creative Commons.

Visit us on the Web!
StepIntoReading.com
rhcbooks.com

Educators and librarians, for a variety of teaching tools, visit us at RHTeachersLibrarians.com

Library of Congress Cataloging-in-Publication Data is available upon request.
ISBN 978-1-5247-7229-1 (trade) — ISBN 978-1-5247-7230-7 (lib. bdg.) — ISBN 978-1-5247-7231-4 (ebook)

Printed in the United States of America
10 9 8 7 6 5 4 3 2 1

First Edition

STEP INTO READING®

STEP 3

READING ON YOUR OWN

A BIOGRAPHY READER

# MICHELLE OBAMA

## First Lady, Going Higher

by Shana Corey

illustrations by James Bernardin

Random House 🏠 New York

This is one of the
most famous
people in the world.

Her name is Michelle Obama.
She is a lawyer.
She is a mother.
And she is the first
African American First Lady
of the United States of America.
But she hasn't always been famous.
In fact, she is a lot like these girls.

Michelle LaVaughn Robinson
was born on the
South Side of Chicago
on January 17, 1964.

Michelle's family didn't have
a lot of money.
They lived in a
one-bedroom apartment.
Michelle and her brother, Craig,
shared a room.

Michelle played
with Barbies.
She took dance lessons.
She rode her bike
and played softball
with her friends.

Her family ate dinners together
and had game nights.
Michelle *hated* to lose!

Michelle's father
had a disease
called multiple sclerosis.
He was often in pain.
Even getting dressed
could be difficult.
But he didn't complain.
He still went to work
every day.

Michelle's parents
taught her and Craig
to aim high and
believe in themselves.
They taught them to get
the best education they could,
then to reach back
and help others.

Michelle was a hard worker.
She skipped second grade
and took extra classes.

She got into a special
high school across town.
She had to travel
more than an hour to get there.

Michelle's brother got
into Princeton University,
one of the best colleges
in America.
Michelle wanted to go
to Princeton, too.

But some of her
high school counselors
said she needed
higher test scores.
Her family didn't have
money for a tutor.
So Michelle worked even harder.

She took advanced classes
and made the honor society.
She sang in choir

and ran track.

She stayed up late
working on college essays,
and she applied for
financial aid.
Michelle's hard work paid off.
She got into Princeton!

When Michelle arrived,
there weren't many
black students at Princeton.
One of her white roommates
changed rooms because
she didn't want a
black roommate.

But Michelle's parents
had taught her not to let
what other people thought
stop her.
She made good friends
and graduated with honors.

Michelle went to
Harvard Law School,
and then got a job
at a law firm in Chicago.
After her first year,
she met a young man
at the firm.
His name was Barack Obama.

Barack was smart and funny,
and he cared about
making a difference in the world.
Michelle and Barack fell in love.

In 1991, Michelle's father died.

Michelle was heartbroken.

She thought about how

her father believed

in reaching back

to help others.

She decided to leave her job

and do just that.

Michelle and Barack were married.
Michelle got a job
helping young people
become leaders.
Later, she worked
at the University of Chicago
helping students volunteer
in the community.

And she and Barack

had two little girls,

Malia and Sasha.

Barack was also working
to help people.

He became a senator.

He wanted to run for

president of the United States,

but only if Michelle agreed.

Michelle knew it would be hard.

But she believed

Barack could make a difference.

She agreed.

America had never had

a black president before.

Michelle traveled all over,

telling people why she thought

Barack would be a good president.

"I'm asking you to stop settling

for the world as it *is*,"

she told people,

"and to help us make the world

as it *should be*."

Barack won the election!
More people voted for him
than for any other candidate
in America's history.

On January 20, 2009,
Barack became the first
African American president
of the United States.
Michelle became the First Lady.

Because she was the first
African American First Lady,
there was a lot of pressure
on Michelle.
Many people
did or said hurtful things
because she was black.
"Remember," she said.
"It's not what people
say about you.
It's what you do."

The White House
was a big change from Chicago.
And being the First Lady
was a big job.
But Michelle said her
most important job was being
Sasha and Malia's mom.
She went to their school events
and tried to make sure the family
ate dinner together.
And she still had the girls
make their own beds.

Michelle wanted to help

America's kids be healthy.

She planted a White House

vegetable garden

and worked to get schools

to offer healthier foods.

She started a program
called Let's Move!
to get kids to be more active.
She Hula-Hooped with them
on the White House lawn.
She danced and
had push-up contests
and potato sack races.
She even dunked a basketball
into a hoop held by
LeBron James!

In 2012, Barack ran
for president again.
Michelle gave a big speech.
She talked about the things
she and Barack
believed in.
She talked about working hard
and helping others
and doing the "impossible."

The audience loved the speech.
And two months later,
Barack was reelected.

For the next four years,
Michelle traveled
all over America.
She started a program
called Reach Higher,
which encouraged kids
to go to college.

She made it her mission
to help girls around the world
go to school.

In her last speech

as First Lady,

Michelle spoke directly

to young people.

"This country belongs to you—

to all of you . . . ," she said.

"Do not ever let anyone

make you feel

like you don't matter . . .

because you do.

And you have a right

to be exactly

who you are."

In 2017, Barack's term
as president ended.
But Michelle wasn't done
helping young people.
On the South Side of Chicago,
not far from where
she grew up,
the Obamas are building
the Obama Presidential Center,
where they will work to inspire
young leaders.
And someday soon . . .
one of those leaders
just might be *you*.